What others are saying about this book:

"In *God's Pencil*, **the author uses her extraordinary way with words to sketch pictures of an awesome God, the wonders of simple pleasures, and all that is sacred and holy.** If you need a spiritual hug or smile, steal away for a few minutes and draw one for yourself with *God's Pencil*."

Andrea Holland, *Director*, Pregnancy Center West

"Mary Pat's poetry delights my faith on every level. The poems range from inspirational to entertaining. Somehow I sense the smile of the *"Author"* behind the *"pencil"* as He reads her heart reflected in these poems. I know my soul smiles with Him. As one who works in the church to build up and inspire fellow Christians and new believers, **I have a great appreciation for works such as this to bless people who are searching for a greater understanding of the Lord and His love for them.**"

Michelle Burke, *Facilitator*, ALPHA Program

"What a treasure! In *God's Pencil*, Mary Pat shares her faith, family memories and personal convictions. Her illuminating poems are written for every occasion. We found ourselves eager to share selections from the treasury of Family poems with the many precious people in our lives. **God's Pencil is a work destined to inscribe a deeper faith on the hearts of all who peruse its pages.**"

James & Mary Gagnon
Teachers/Facilitators RENEW Program

GOD'S PENCIL

SURVIVAL POETRY FOR TODAY'S WORLD

MARY PAT STRENGER LOOMIS

Forever Blessings —
Pat and Al
Mary Pat

FIRST EDITION

MUSTARD SEED WORDS, BALTIMORE, MARYLAND

GOD'S PENCIL

SURVIVAL POETRY FOR TODAY'S WORLD

By Mary Pat Strenger Loomis

Published by:

mustard seed words
The tiny Christian press with the rich rewards
P. O. Box 6340 • Baltimore, MD 21230

Some poems contain references to Scripture. As these works are paraphrased and not used verbatim, permission is not required from a specific translation.

Printed in the United States of America

ISBN 0-9665608-4-1
Library of Congress Catalog Card Number 98-067169

*Dedicated
to my
faith-filled parents
and
to my children,
Luke and Therese
and all those who,
by nature or choice,
have been denied a birthday.*

You are not forgotten.

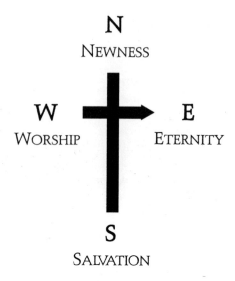

Your compass for the journey …

Table of Contents

I Inspirational

II Nature

III Family

Foreword

No less a personage than Mother Teresa of Calcutta is supposed to have said once, "I feel like a pencil in God's hand; no matter how poor the instrument the handwriting is always beautiful." Unaware of the quote, Mary Pat chose a title using the same image, a pencil. Maybe there's a similar kind of holiness in Mary Pat. Maybe Mother Teresa had something of the poet within her.

Whatever the case regarding the title image, there's no mistaking other striking parallel themes in the lives of these two kindred spirits: the splendor of God's presence in every human and every human experience; the sparkling joy of the gift of children; the horror of abortion; the value of suffering and the mountainous trust in God that enables one to see Him at play throughout the universe.

Add to this Mary Pat's touching portraits of family members, her depth of feeling about the mysteries of her faith, the resonance she feels with mothers and martyrs, sinners and saints, makes this little volume an inspiration and a delight.

Rev. Francis A. Sirolli, O.S.A.

Preface

Why *God's Pencil*? Many of these prayers/poems flowed from me with little effort, the result of prayerfully asking for words that would make a difference. I feel like a simple tool (that's *t* not *f!*) the Lord has used, therefore, *God's Pencil*.

Some are the poetical development of insights that finally penetrated the cranium, and a few are the celebration of goodness and Godness graced in nature and family.

However, they all reflect *my* experience of God; through my relationship with Him as a Catholic daughter, mother, and disciple. Though we experience God in different ways, I hope you can relate to these. I hope they touch your life in a positive, challenging way. We all have the potential to be instruments of God; not only His pencils, but His paintbrushes, His guitars, His hammers. We should not only allow, but prayerfully ask of ourselves to be used. For *how* we survive today's world will surely determine the next.

Acknowledgment

This book would not have been ready until the *next* millenium, if it were not for the generous efforts of the following people. I thank them sincerely for their eyeballs, their shoulders, their brain cells and their treasure, with special appreciation for the technical assistance of my patient father-in-law, Raymond Loomis, Sr. *God bless you all!*

Vince and Pat Strenger
Ray and Rose Loomis
Roy Loomis
Timothy, Elizabeth & Nicholas Loomis
Clare Strenger
Roseann Loomis Burkhardt
Rev. Francis Sirolli, O.S.A.
Rev. Bill Mannion, Jr.
Cliff and Joan Hargadon
Jamie and Mary Gagnon
Susan Fetcho
Mike and Michelle Burke
Jim Noonan
Dan Mountney
Raymond Loomis, Jr.
Frank and Rose Miller
Catherine Dix
Ted Schargel
Mike Fuka
Connie Southerington

Cover Design by Mary Pat Strenger Loomis
Cover Art by Roseann Loomis Burkhardt

About the Author

Mary Pat Strenger Loomis is a native of Philadelphia, the fourth child in a family of eight, which inspired much of her poetry from an early age. She attributes her strong faith to a gift from God which was richly nourished by her parents and her Catholic education.

Transplanted to Baltimore in 1988 with her husband, she is the mother of three, a former foster mom to six and a former day-care mom to dozens.

She works part-time at the family's print shop and as a freelance writer (*"Now I know why they call it free!"*) Her experience as a volunteer counselor at a crisis pregnancy center is reflected in much of her writing.

While searching for a publisher, Mary Pat felt God's nudging to establish her own Christian publishing house. She is now the founder of Mustard Seed Words — *the tiny Christian press with rich rewards*. She is currently working on a children's book and is looking forward to planting more *mustard seeds*.

I

Inspirational

In all I do, may I serve You.

Majestic Mercy

He scatters stars like sugar,
He assumes our tiny flaws;

He sets the waves a rockin',
He repairs His broken laws.

He gives life to every creature,
He forgives life's sorry foes;

For equal to His majesty
*Is the mercy that He shows!**

*Based on Sirach 2:18

Echo

When friends betray,
When it's time to pray,
May I echo You;

When faith they scorn,
For treasure mourn,
May I echo You;

When anger bursts,
Compassion thirsts,
When a life can not be free;

May I echo You
In all I do,
That they might echo me.

Heart of Gold

Help me to remember, Lord,
When suffering seems unfair,
You test our faith, you test our strength,
You test how much we care.

As the test of gold is fire,*
Letting purity unfold,
You take our spirit, try to clear it,
And forge a heart of gold.

Based on Zech. 13:9

Alm Psalm

Raphael gave a message
To Tobit long ago,
For life to own, for sins atone,
Alms you must bestow.

Prayer and fasting are worthy ways,
But they don't cost a dime;
Talk is cheap and frequent fasting
Trims the old waistline.

If you want to live forever,
Give from what you'd keep;
Let no one know the good you sow
And God's bounty you will reap.*

Based on Tobit 12:8-9

Hearts Don't Know Miles

Though oceans stretch between us
And mountains shield our eyes,
We are still connected —
Still have natural ties.

The same sun starts our days,
One moon tucks us in;
We share one God wherever we trod,
Our souls forever kin.

So joyfully kick the moon to us
As we shove the sun your way;
And God will keep our spirits one
Every time we pray.

Happy Birthday Jesus

To celebrate His birthday
Simplicity is best;
A heartfelt prayer, love to share
Would please this honored Guest.

Sing a song, bake a cake,
Cater to each whim;
In any amount, the thought does count —
Just remember Him.

Reached

Reached by foot, reached by hand,
Reached by bended knee;
Reached by camel, reached by boat,
Reached by climbing tree.

Reached through fire, reached through wind,
Reached through drops of sea;
Reached through prayer, reached through song,
Reached through history.

Reached in silence, reached in pain,
Reached in ministry;
Reached in words, reached in Bread,
Reached inside of me.

Heartwork

My grandpop used to tell me
On every Christmas Eve,
The animals would bow in praise
Then humbly take their leave.

As soulless as they're thought to be
They have a knowing heart;
For big or small, they're struck with awe —
We're each His work of art.

A Star is Born

Today I see the outside world
And hear My mother's voice;
Presented by My Father —
Hear the world rejoice!

Although I'm safe and know the plan,
I feel a little scared;
I've got to stay and show the way
As no one ever dared.

Will they listen? Will they learn,
How to be truly happy?
I gift Myself — just lift Myself
And joyously unwrap Me!

Drummer Boy

I hear the beat of a single drum,
A pure and simple pace,
Expressing joy of one small boy,
One small human race.

I hear the beat of a thousand hearts
Sounding out a call:
Come rejoice! Join our voice —
Peace to one and all.

Star of Light

Star of wonder, star of light,
Fill our homes and make them bright;
Light each pane and soul we see,
Illuminate with love of Thee.

Brighten hearts and hearths as one,
Powered by the brilliant Son;
Shine through wind and rain and snow,
Glow, let it glow, let it glow!

Calm and Bright

If just for this season
Create corners of calm,
Not red-eyed exhaustion
Just absence of qualm.

If just for this season
Go do something bright!
Not golden and glittered
But filled with delight!

If just for this season
Welcome each morn,
It's just for these reasons
The Child was born.

Soular System

Look directly into the Son —
You will reflect the shine;
Look directly into the Son
And never more be blind.

Look directly into the Son —
Be warmed down to your toes;
Look directly into the Son
And melt away your woes.

Look directly into the Son —
Heat your heart to the brim;
Look directly into the Son —
You will revolve around Him.

Mary Had a Little Lamb

Each birth renews an age-old hope,
Each birth creates much joy;
Each birth gifts us another chance
To love the Jesus boy.

With gentleness so strongly seen,
With innocence so wise,
With purity of heart and mind
They help us realize:

This begins our journey home —
This truth will never dim;
For Mary had a little Lamb
So we could follow Him.

God's Toybox

He drop-kicks the sun,
Ping-pongs the moon,
Mother Earth's His dreidel.
The Grand Canyon is His soup pot,
The Big Dipper – His ladle.

Does He dive-bomb hawk and buzzard?
Holster shooting stars?
Cuddle with a grizzly?
Putt planets under par?

I know His wit and playful puns,
I know His restful day;
For this Father, it's no bother
To take the time to play.

How Does Your Garden Grow?

I've planted myself
in your garden;
to bask
in your sweet sunshine,
to drink
from your fountain of knowledge,
to be strengthened
by your evergreen faith.

So often
I've walked your garden steps —
you never latch the gate.
Within your walls
I'm uplifted,
refreshed.
You are the place I go
to bloom.

Bird of Pray

More than just another bird,
More than wind and flame,
You heal my soul and answer me
Each time I call Your name.

I know the Father, know the Son,
I used to pass You by —
Low man on the totem pole
Not even worth a try.

Oh Great Mover, Wondrous Shaker,
You bring to life His word;
I hang my head for times I said
You were just another bird.

Walking Trinity

Today God let me see
With natural simplicity
A walking breathing trinity.

One body met my eye,
Three hearts passed me by,
Three souls did edify.

The parallel of origins
Where the mystery begins
One young mother having twins.

Prayer Before the Doors

Holy Spirit empty me,
With the cross of water cleanse;
Prepare me for the feast within
Erase my whats and whens.

Overflow my ears with Word,
Place Bread upon my tongue;
Help me grasp my brother's hand,
Feel each song that's sung.

Let me breathe Your fragrance sweet,
Help me see Your face;
Fill me through each sense, Oh Lord,
Fill me full of grace.

Heart Burn

Reverent hymn, soulful song,
Voice undisciplined;
Every breath I take for Him
Feeds the fire within.

Joyful noise, praising psalm,
Freedom unrestrained;
Energy coursing within me,
Feet are uncontained.

Ancient words, holding true,
Words that red men bring:
God respects me when I work
*But He loves me when I sing!**

*Based on Indian wisdom

First Eucharist

You came to His table today
Yearning to be fed;
Scrubbed heart and soul,
then were made whole
Receiving holy Bread.

Grace poured in, love shone through,
You quenched a holy thirst;
Let every Eucharist you receive
Be as special as the first.

Full of Life

Jesus is alive in me
When I taste the Bread and bow;
Mary carried Jesus then,
I transport Him now.

Unbreaking #2

The dock is teeming,
Your Name they're screaming,
A quiet man tips his hat.
They bang their thumb
And curse Your Son —
Again, he comes to bat.

A mother is strolling,
The wheels stop rolling,
Someone's hollered, *"Christ!"*
She takes the swear,
Makes it a prayer —
A silent sacrifice.

A child is playing,
Someone is saying
"Jesus Lord above!"
He bows his head
Each time it's said,
This Name he's learned to love.

Strange gods

Zenith, Sony, Emerson,
IBM, Macintosh,
Aerosmith, Rolling Stones,
Claiborne, Klein, Osh-Kosh,

Washington, Franklin, Jackson, Grant,
Sega, NES,
Orioles, Eagles, Flyers, Bulls,
President, Baroness,

Heineken, Gallo, J&B,
Valium, LSD,
Mercedes, Porsche, Excalibur,
Compuserve, Prodigy.

Today I Met The Pope

Never feeling nervous,
I waited eagerly;
Reviewed my list, kept the gist,
Of things not meagerly.

I brought the prayers and piercing pain
Of those I left behind;
I was people, places, a thousand faces,
A jigsaw of mankind.

He came among us quietly,
My heart saw before my eyes;
Our holy Pope, vested in hope,
Seemed patient, loving, wise.

A ripple of peace spread through us,
Truly love at first sight;
I felt maternal, and joy eternal,
A heady sensation of flight.

He touched my hands, he touched my heart,
He looked into my eyes;
He gifted me, he lifted me,
His words I memorized.

I doubt he will remember me,
I have no claim to fame;
But I feel holy, I feel whole,
And I'll never be the same.

Soul Survivors

Remove the bodies, get more sand —
Lay the floor with fresh;
The last has drunk its fill of blood
And bits of mangled flesh.

Christian, slave, or wild beast —
Remains all look the same;
Titus got his money's worth —
The public loves the game.

Unseen are soulless shadows
That paint each corridor;
Unheard are pain and prayer and anguish
Locked beneath the floor.

Silent cries, eternal screams,
Repoint each crumbling stone;
The martyr mortar slowly sets
An emperor's new throne.

Generations will always feel
The horror there within;
For each arched vault their hearts assault:
"Let the games begin."

Catholicism

The meaning of my Catholic faith
Has varied through my life;
A child knows a Father's love,
His guidance as mom and wife.

Guardian angels protect me,
Saints listen and inspire;
Nuns and priests live their faith
And help me to strive higher.

Ten Commandments guide me,
And a Book of wondrous riches;
Sacraments for grace and peace
Whenever my conscience itches.

Through faith I see the good in bad,
I don't think much of *things*,
I know it's right, with all my might,
I love the joy it brings!

Life Glue

To mend a cracked and broken heart,
To rebuild a bridge you've burned,
To reinforce a weakened bond,
To hold a soul you've spurned,

To repair a shattered ego,
To strengthen more than new
Life's fragile reconstructions —
"I'm sorry" is the glue.

Forgiveness

Daily I do make mistakes
And fail to hold my tongue;
Misjudge an act or stranger's face,
Leave praises quite unsung.

Then my heart starts aching,
Longing to be healed;
So ashamed to cause such pain,
Grateful hearts aren't sealed.

"I am truly sorry,"
Is all I need to say,
To heal my stinging monster words,
To wash the weight away.

Forgiveness wraps around me,
His smile reaffirms
That I am loved with all my faults
And fabricated terms.

I breathe this into memory
For next when *I* am pained,
I'll forgive *their* sorry heart,
Exhale away their chain.

Counseled by the Holy Book
As the truest way to live,
We shall be forgiven
In the measure we forgive.*

Based on Mt. 6:12

II

Nature

Perfect Morn

God had just popped the seal
On a crisp, fresh, morn.
Dew stars twinkled, clouds unwrinkled,
Moonflowers worn.

Life at rest, babe at breast,
Honeysuckle scent;
Cardinals flying, breezes sighing,
Moments merely lent.

Windowed in another world,
Uplifted, overawed;
Uncompared, the gift was shared,
I watched the leaves applaud.

Wash Out

Sun on my face,
Wind in my hair,
I pin each dampened sheet.

They soak up the sun,
They filter the wind,
Like fields of flannel wheat.

My face on the sun,
My hair on the wind,
Sleep is oh so sweet!

Dancing Rainbows

When an August sun arrives for brunch
He's set on ice with glee!
Suspended in his crystal cage
He's twirled expectantly.

Rainbows waltz across the wall
And leap upon the ceiling;
Twist across the table top,
Start Virginia reeling!

They two-step by two tiny feet,
Perform a pelvic prance,
Shimmy on a short sleeve shirt,
Begin a belly dance.

'Round and 'round and 'round they fly
Until the sun breaks free —
Returning through the windows west
Just in time for tea!

Aqua Footsie

I wriggle my toes in the sand,
Warm by the end of the day,
Patiently waiting for lapping waves
To tickle the sand away.

Gold Fever

I watch as the sun
Splashes gold on the sea,
And I step even closer
Hoping some lands on me.

Stone Pigeons

He scrutinized each stony path,
Sifted through a pile,
Surprised a slumbering slimy slug —
Borrowed his bed for awhile.

Gray stones were the ones preferred,
Streaked with white the best;
A rounded base, a bumpy head,
Would be his shoebox guest.

He gathered close to himself
All the newly hatched;
One young boy with nature's toy
Had words to be dispatched.

Little scraps of ragged notes
Coded as in Greek,
Were wrapped around a granite leg —
The legless, 'round a beak.

Each stone was cupped in dried mud palms
Wrapped snug with fingers five;
Engulfed in dreams and young boy warmth
The birds emerged alive!

They flew with speed of baseball fame
Into a friend's back yard;
Waited for a message swap —
Flew homeward fast and hard.

He carefully unwrapped each note,
Then cleaned and dried each bird;
Scattered tiny pebble feed,
Talked without a word.

Nestled in the coop from Keds,
Beneath an early moon,
He tucked them in with discipline,
They cooed a goodnight tune.

Summer Snow

Cottonwoods sigh
Their soft babies down;
Miniature clouds
To cushion the ground.

They whiten our toes,
They blanket bare skin;
We kick with abandon
As fluff reaches shin!

Fistfuls are flung
In faces with glee,
Armfuls are swooped
In sheer ecstasy!

We had come for a cone
From *The Candy Box* minter,
But were much more refreshed
With her serving of Winter.

III

Family

Miracle Control

My life was always in control —
This birth would be the same;
We'll have one in a couple years,
Time to pick a name!

Okay, I think we're ready now,
Let's plan for one in May.
I'll stop the pill — what a thrill!
Let nature lead the way.

May is here. May is gone.
Three calendars mock my soul.
Something's wrong with nature's song —
I have lost control.

Babies, babies, everywhere;
They spit them out like seeds,
So wondrous and extraordinary
My inner voice concedes.

Children are a gift from God,*
Sings psalm so lyrical,
And who am I, to even try,
Preventing such a miracle?

*Based on Psalm 127:3

Unborn Song

I don't know when it happened —
It started as a hum;
A song was taking shape inside
Waiting to be sung.

Hole notes and foot notes,
Buds before the bloom,
Wrapped safe inside a manuscript
Of a calming, rhythmic womb.

Months and months I nurtured
This kicking melody;
Wrote in pauses, extra rests,
When the need would be.

I couldn't wait to share my song —
Oh, what joy I'd bring!
So unique, I couldn't speak,
It was all so humbling.

I labored hours, I sweated seas,
I heard that first sweet cry!
With a symphony of effort
I'd composed a lullaby.

Could Have Beens

He could have been

a writer,
a soldier,
a curer of ills,

a teacher,
a preacher,
a drafter of wills,

a printer,
a daddy,
some new history;

But each non-born child's
one more mystery.

Abortion

Quick fix.
Bad time —
I need to be free.

A little time,
A little green —
This is history.

She thrashed inside!
Oh, God, they lied!
This should never be!

Every little piece of her
Took all the peace in me.

Can't sleep.
Can't eat.
Always, always crying.

Now my little girl is free
But I'm forever dying.

Silent Cry

    swish
I like my little room,
    swish
It's dark and peaceful here,
  swish
I float about quite pleasantly,
The Special One is near.

I hear when she makes music —
    swish
It makes me want to flip!
    swish
I wonder when I'll meet her . . .
    swish
I think she is a ship.

I hear her steady motor
Always thump-thump-thump,
At times when it goes really fast
I bump-bump-bump!

I guess I'm just too little
To meet her or the sun,
My tiny feet could find a seat
On the nail of someone's thumb.

Oh! The motor's really racing!
I feel like something's wrong!
Special One, please help me!
Sing a pretty song.

There's something coming near me!
I move from side to side!
It tracks me! It whacks me!
There's no place I can hide.

It's sucking off my arm!
It's really hurting me!
Someone get the Special One!
Now it's got my knee!

It's sucking off my leg!
It's coming towards my head!
I'm sucked inside! My parts collide!
I fear I'll soon be

Most Selfless Mother

For whatever reason,
She came at the wrong season,
You knew she couldn't stay.

You searched heart and soul —
Joy was the toll,
Bravely you gave her away.

We praise you for your loving heart,
God's grace will fill the empty part —
His blessings overflow.

Every day your child lives,
Every joy your child gives,
Is because you loved her so.

No Carriage

You returned to Jesus
Before I saw your face;
Why did He take you back —
Withdraw His gift of grace?

Was He short an angel,
Or had you claimed His heart?
A reason would console me —
Fill the empty part.

The weeks you grew inside me
I spent knitting dreams;
Now I see how fragile
My forever seems.

When clouds part to welcome me
No longer must I wait;
My heart will surely find you
Swinging heaven's gate.

Moon Babies

Gone before his birthing time.
I feel the need to plant.
I handle unfamiliar seeds —
Bury — but I can't.

The packet reads *Moonflowers*,
They stay awake all night;
Babies of the moon, think I,
He understands my plight.

They wander and they wrap themselves
Around the garden fence;
Exploring parts, gathering hearts,
Clothed in innocence.

They draw admiring glances,
Neighbors *ooh* and *aah*,
From a tiny sprig they've grown so big —
I feel the proud ma-ma.

They stop for frozen custard
Before their big night out;
They open wide with naught to hide,
Each pure and radiant sprout.

Their fragrance calls at tub time,
I inhale as it grows louder;
Stuns my soul, makes me whole,
Perfumed in baby powder.

A Mother's Lap

For sleeping,
for dreaming,
for healing,
for love;

For safety,
for comfort,
for journeys above;

For reading,
for rocking,
for pat-a-cake glee;

Mom's is the lap
Of pure luxury.

My Irish Mother

My Irish mother smells of soap,
Of violets in the morn,
Of buttermilk that's thick and fresh,
Of a day that's newly born.

My Irish mother sounds like song —
Humming as she reaps;
Chopping to a Celtic beat,
Waltzing as she sweeps.

She looks angelic, so serene,
Donning coats of cheer;
Her skin unwrinkled as a pearl,
Her frock of faith sincere.

So soothing and refreshing,
A haven safe — with tea!
With unconditional love like His
She feels like heaven to me.

My Mom Could Never Be A Flower

If my mom were a flower
She'd be a classic rose —
Timeless and elegant,
Pleasing eye and nose.

Magical! Spontaneous!
Like the changing dandelion,
So much fun to play with,
Sending laughter flyin'!

Or, perhaps, a pretty crocus
With colors all aglow,
Surprising! Optimistic!
Pushing cheerily through the snow.

Or a pure and spiritual lily
Whose heart you cannot harden;
No, my mom could never be a flower —
She's too much of a garden.

Rose

We have found the perfect rose
Quite unexpectedly,
Full of color, free of thorn,
Blooms eternally.

The brightest little pick-me-up,
A natural soothing balm;
Radiating joy complete,
We tagged the beauty *Mom*.

Pop-Pop

You are the only grandpop I knew,
Or remember knowing;

Mom says you liked daffodils —
So I plant some,
to remember.

Mom says you worked at Horn & Hardharts —
So I hang their pie plate,
to remember.

I used to kneel and giggle to Radio Rosary
And you understood a child's way.
Now I pray the beads with my son,
to remember.

I fought with Clare over pushing buttons;
(Marie Ward said *I* could),
Your gentle scolding showed you cared,
So I push a button,
to remember.

These days I watch my daughter with my dad,
And each special moment
Affords me the chance
to remember to remember.

Memories of Nan-Nan

Coming home after school
Was such a fragrant treat;
Soda bread or wheaten loaves
Were waiting warm and sweet.

I had the eye of a traveling rat,
Was your poetic view;
And as a pinochle partner
None compared with you.

Many nights I stayed in town
And caught the last train out;
You always waited up for me —
A worried faithful scout.

You were always glad to see me,
Read my poems to each friend;
Approved my loft apartment,
Had energy without end.

Are you making snowflakes now?
Or weaving willow wings?
Playing your harmonica
While angels pluck their strings?

Through the art you've left behind
I feel your strength and love,
And know you're waiting, watching still,
From the cleanest cloud above.

Nan-Nan's Teapot

Roses grown on 'C' Street
Your teapot decorate;
Like cups of wine and bowls of blush —
Gold trim a touch ornate.

Worn and polished by your hands
Safe-keeping family lore;
Companion to your soda bread
And love that would outpour.

The gold has somehow saved your face,
Reflections from each brew;
And it comforts me, that I can see,
I'm having tea with you.

Daddy Oak

Dad, you've stood the test of time
Like a stoic giant oak;
Imparting strength of values
My spirit can't unyoke.

Your shady humor brings relief
From all the world's hot air;
Each branch of love supports me,
Each leaf is veined in prayer.

Eight acorns have you scattered,
Our roots of faith entwine;
You will always be a part of me
And all that I design.

I thank Our Father for my father,
A blessing so sublime;
Through the cheers and through the tears
You've stood the test of time.

My Chair Man

Soft and thickly padded,
A lap to curl upon,
A respite from a busy dày,
To plan my future on.

My dad is like my favorite chair —
A place I feel secure;
And every time I settle there,
I seem to love it more.

Bankers Make the Best Dads

Thanks for always teaching me
I'm *rich* beyond my years,
For putting *interest* in my accounts
For *lending* me your ears.

For showing me to use *common cents*
Whenever my *balance* sank,
And for making so many priceless *deposits*
Direct to my memory bank.

Aunt Madge

As children do
We tested you —
Made faces to your face.

"How blind is blind?
The light she'll find"!
You found the Light of grace.

When siblings teased
You always eased
My spirits in a slump;

You said it firm —
The proper term
For her is *pleasingly plump*.

I stuck out my tongue
With that song you sung —
Then a thought warmed like a glove:

If you are blind,
And love is blind,
Then Aunt Madge, you must be love.

Suzanne

A great success, to my mind,
Isn't found from nine-to-five;
For chairman or vice-president
Are simple things to strive.

Try making multiple decisions
While cooking a healthy meal,
Or refereeing a scuffle
From behind the steering wheel.

Or talking to your banker
While the cord becomes a rope,
Or prevent an infant's drowning
When she's slippery with soap.

Can they answer 100 questions
Every hour of the day?
Organize eight wardrobes
And still find time to play?

Can they cheer the team, bake a cake,
Sew and scrub and sweep?
Do they set aside some time for God
When God knows they need the sleep?

Can they stretch a buck, drive a van,
Remember special days?
Sometimes work outside the home?
Have time to praise? Amaze?

My sister does these beautifully —
Drug-free and still alive;
And if she ever needs a rest
She'll land a nine-to-five.

Singing Sisters

We used to sing ourselves to sleep
Awaiting Santa's sleigh;
And sing assorted sudsy songs
Storing dinner plates away.

We sung and swung on playground swings
And the steps of Old Grace Church;
We boogied and bellowed around the globe
From a tropical island perch.

As sisters go — you've never gone,
We'll never be apart;
Through thick and thin, through lose or win,
You keep a song in my heart!

Guardian Angel

A presence watches over me,
Converses with each thought,
Nudges me down prudent paths,
Shows me things I sought.

Bolsters my self-confidence,
Soothes an aching heart,
Keeps me out of trouble,
Appreciates God-art.

Smooths a lonesome wrinkled brow
And urges me to dare;
When skies are pink, I sometimes think,
My guardian is Clare.

Sea Isle

A wagon overflowing
Travels mile after mile;
Crammed with kids and happy cries
Headed for Sea Isle.

Each nose vacations first
As it sniffs the salty sea;
We pull into twenty seven
Killeen as Killeen can be!
One half block to aqua glory —
To somersault the surf;
To own our private castle,
To tread its ticklish turf.

An outdoor shower, an awesome lunch,
Readies us for boards;
A crucial stop at Copper Kettle —
We're now amusement lords!

Aunt Agnes bids good-bye in brogue,
We each hug Ann Marie;
Then stumble to the loaded car
To relive the reverie.

A wagon overflowing
Travels back a hundred miles;
Stuffed with spreads and sleepy heads,
Sunburn, sand and smiles.

The Mitchell Farm

We visited cousins (older than mom!)
On a real-live Jersey farm;
The cows filed in, greeted like kin,
By a long mechanical arm.

Their stomachs were pumped as they dined unaware
Amid the straw and the dirt;
A bowl set aside, where kittens might hide,
Was given a generous squirt.

We climbed a rubber mountain wide
Energized with milk;
Hitched a tractor ride to a place to hide
Dressed in pure corn silk.

Three little brothers in a hay loft high
Were looking rather cute;
I snapped my lens before those wrens
Flew off in hot pursuit.

Simple features, gentle creatures,
A peaceful habitat —
A farm might not be truly heaven
But at least, the welcome mat.

Christmas Visitors

Earl Grey is steeping anxiously,
The children can't be heard;
The china's on the table
Waiting for a word.

Each day brings some surprises —
A friend from overseas!
New babies in the family,
News and recipes.

The porch emits a jingle,
I rush to see who's there;
I bring in three or four or more
And park them in a chair.

I take my time and savor each
Reunion through a pen;
Then I fill up another cup
And read each card again.

Family Tree

My family tree's my Christmas tree,
Standing full and strong;
Linking all in garland hugs,
Bellowing yuletide song.

Angels climb and somersault,
Ringing laughter bells;
Father Christmas in the kitchen
Tasting Christmas smells.

The sparkle in so many eyes,
The glow on every face,
The radiance of happy hearts
Reflects His loving grace.

Gifts in varied shapes and sizes,
Wrinkled wrapping worn,
Precious parcels tumbling out,
Their paper newly born.

The strengths of our past, the hopes of our future,
Lie within our ken;
And whenever we're together
It's Christmas time again.

Coming Home To You

Sometimes the morning parting
Leaves my throat a little tight;
Your wave and tender smile
Are the last I'll see 'til night.
The pain is bittersweet
But it's worth going through,
Beause it feels so good
Coming home to you.

Between the crazy rush hours
Is a hectic nine-to-five;
I stand alone in mindless crowds
Then your face comes to mind.
I start anticipating
The things we're going to do,
And it keeps me sane —
Coming home to you.

I see your silhouette
In the porch light's dusky glow,
Running down to greet me,
Arms stretching *hello;*
My pace begins to quicken,
My heart just skips a few,
Beause it feels so good
Coming home to you.

In Search of a Poem

There's one on every child's face,
On every broken heart;
One in every pair of hands,
Every piece of art.

There's some in every act of God
And every act of man;
There's some in everything that grows,
Some in every clan.

There are thousands in the moon and stars,
Thousands in the sea,
Thousands in the sun and sky
But all inside of me.

ORDERING INFORMATION

To order a copy of this book, please send $9.95 plus $3.00 shipping & handling to:

Mustard Seed Words
P. O. Box 6340-A
Baltimore, MD 21230

(You may order up to 4 copies @ $9.95 each with one shipping cost of $3.00). Orders shipped to a Maryland address please add 5%.)

Any groups interested in ordering more than 4 copies please contact us for discount rates:

(410) 644-3046   FAX: (410) 837-6060

A major portion of the proceeds are donated to pro-life causes.

If you would like a copy of this book and can not afford it, just send what you can and one will be mailed to you.

In His service,

Mary Pat Strenger Loomis